THE CHANGING MEANING OF FEMINISM

Life Cycle and Career Implications
from a Sociological Perspective

Susan Louise Peterson

International Scholars Publications
San Francisco - London - Bethesda
1998

Library of Congress Cataloging-in-Publication Data

Peterson, Susan Louise, 1960-
    The changing meaning of feminism : life cycle and career
    implications from a sociological perspective / Susan Louise
    Peterson.
      p. cm.
    Includes index

    ISBN 1-57309-306-8 (alk. paper). -- ISBN 1-57309-305-X
    (pbk. : alk. paper)
    1. Feminism--United States--History. 2. Women--United States-
    -Social conditions. 3. Women--Employment--United States. 4. Women-
    -United States--Economic conditions. 5. Marriage--United States.
    I. Title.
    HQ1154.P4295   1998
    305.42'0973--dc21   98-16519
                                         CIP

Editorial Inquiries:
International Scholars Publications
7831 Woodmont Avenue, #345
Bethesda, MD 20814

To order: (800) 55-PUBLISH

Dedicated to
Alan
my egalitarian
dual career marriage partner
(PS It's been wonderful!)

TABLE OF CONTENTS

ILLUSTRATIONS

FOREWORD

Research in women's studies and feminism has broadened and deepened as women move through life stages, shedding new light on old issues facing women. Still, as Dr. Peterson writes in this book, it is extremely difficult to define feminism. From her perspective as an educator and sociologist, she eloquently defines the changing meaning of feminism as it relates to a woman's life cycle changes and her own personal growth.

Even the word feminism stirs up emotions and controversy. In her many years of teaching and research, Dr. Peterson discovered that she was not alone in her search for the changing meaning of feminism. To make sense of it, she explores the many types of feminists, choices, challenges, roles, and stereotypes. Here, we have a chance to look at feminism from a variety of perspectives, allowing us the opportunity to examine our own life cycle changes and how we fit in with what she refers to as the "ever-changing cycle of feminism."

In my work as the director of a university women's center, I recognize the importance of research, which helps us understand our past and prepares us for the future. In chapter eight, titled *Spreading the Message of Feminism,* Dr. Peterson offers us a challenge, by listing more than 75 topics and ideas relating to feminism that could be researched and explored to gain a better understanding of feminism.

The Changing Meaning of Feminism is an opportunity to revisit feminism with a new attitude of tolerance, understanding, and celebration for the many varied and significant contributions women make in society. I commend Dr. Peterson for her efforts to keep feminism alive.

Conee L. Spano, Director
Jean Nidetch Women's Center, University of Nevada, Las Vegas

PREFACE

The Changing Meaning of Feminism is one of the most refreshing books that I have read recently. Susan Louise Peterson's search for the definition of feminism has brought her full circle in her understanding of feminism. Feminism has been a part of women's lives for nearly a hundred years, but only played a major role for many of us within the past thirty years. The feminist movement was needed to help raise the conscious level of women's rights in our country, but for many women the feminist movement caused feelings of guilt or confusion. Most of the women that I work with are considered displaced homemakers or are women who have been institutionalized within the prison system. Their views of feminism are very different from those of women who choose to continue their education or work outside their homes. Now that their situations have changed and they need to enter the job market, they must look at their definition of feminism and the rights of women. Ms. Peterson's book can help us understand that each woman has the right to define feminism in her own way.

Desireé A. Dones, Program Manager & Women's Training Consultant

ACKNOWLEDGMENTS

I would like to thank the many individuals who inspired me to fulfill my goal of writing this book. First, I would like to thank the many men and women professors, colleagues, friends and students who helped me gain insights into women's studies and understand the different angles and points of view that make up the perspectives of women. I do not remember all of your names, but I remember how your ideas and visions helped me to re-evaluate my thinking about feminism.

I would like to thank Joan Sanders for her help in the manuscript preparation and her ever patient support of my writing projects. Thanks to the editorial board of International Scholars Publications who believed that it was time to share some changing ideas about feminism with the world.

Finally, to my husband Alan, I give a heartfelt appreciation for his patience, love and support as I learned and explored the study of feminism during our marriage. He knows this is a continual process as I re-examine the changing meaning of feminism.

INTRODUCTION

As a young college professor teaching sociology and human relations courses it was inevitable that the topic of feminism would come up in class. Of course, at the tender age of twenty-six I responded back to the students promptly with my viewpoint about women as if I had all of the answers. Ten years later I began to re-examine my viewpoint as I tried to put some kind of meaning to the term feminism. During this time my own personal ideas about feminism were in a flux of change. I began to question myself and my life choices related to feminism.

My interest level on feminism seemed to waver as I found myself in different social and academic situations. Sometimes my feelings about feminism were strong and determined and at other times I did not even think about feminism. Something inside me kept drawing me back to this subject. I began to question whether I personally identified with other women who called themselves feminists? Had marriage and family life changed my views about feminism? In mid-life, I felt a great need to explore feminism again. Where did I fit in as part of the ever-changing cycle of feminism? This book explores a variety of life experiences that have helped me to understand and put the changing meaning of feminism into perspective. It is hoped that this book will help you clarify and raise questions and issues in your search for meaning in feminism.

I wish I could say that feminism is not a controversial subject. It would be so easy if it were a subject that could be summarized and explained in step by step instructions. Feminism is a topic that stirs both men and women as they untangle their web of emotions. Women think about their past experiences and how they have been treated by others. They remember their childhood events, family habits, dating and marriage relationships and how these things were part of establishing their identity. These social situations greatly affect the views that many women have about feminism. Women's views change about feminism as life cycle events occur and education alters their beliefs about how women should and do behave and what they can accomplish. My purpose in writing *The Changing Meaning of Feminism* is to search for an understanding in the changing world of feminism from a sociological perspective. By understanding how and why the meaning of feminism changes, women can gain insight into why feminism remains a controversial topic.

One afternoon, I was talking to the custodian at work and I happened to mention that I was writing a book on feminism. He seemed so surprised as he commented, "You do not act like a feminist," and "I never thought you were one of those." I began to wonder how people think about feminists. Do they suppose that women who believe in some aspect of feminism all act and think the same way? Did the custodian visualize me as a woman who refused to do dishes or cook a meal? Maybe he saw me as a woman who challenged his ego or made more money than he did. I wondered about all the things that went through his mind when he heard me say the word 'feminism.' Were his notions about feminism based on family tradition or was he filled with anger from his failed marriage and divorce experience? Whatever the case, he made me aware that many people feel that feminists are a small group of women with a narrow focus that behave a certain way. I feel that the world of feminism is filled with a wide array of women who have unique viewpoints, but share some similar concerns.

Best Wishes,
Susan Louise Peterson, Ph.D.

CHAPTER ONE
MAKING SENSE OF FEMINISM

DEFINING FEMINISM

I really believe that no one person could answer all the questions I have about feminism. Like most things, each individual must reflect on his or her ideas and put a topic like feminism in perspective. If you label yourself as a feminist, you will usually be bombarded with people's negative past memories and emotions about women. You will start hearing stories about how a mother neglected her children by taking a job and going to school to study for a career. Still others will share about broken marriages and how a spouse left him once she took a job outside the home. It is not as if you are going to tell the world you are a feminist and they are going to stand up and applaud you. The opposite is usually true. If you are identified as a feminist you will be questioned as if you should understand the history of women and the entire field of women's studies. The parties you use to enjoy will turn into major battlegrounds as differences of opinion never seem to be resolved. Some of the feminist issues you will be questioned on will lose focus in the discussion as bias and stereotypes creep into the conversation. Women have received so much flack about being "a feminist" that many of them do not want to be labeled or even connected with feminist ideas. They may agree with some points a feminist makes, but many choose not to become involved with groups that identify themselves as feminists. These women want to maintain their own individual ideas about what it means to be a woman and express their own concerns about women in society.

As I mentioned earlier, feminism is not that easy of a term to define. However, as author of this book, I feel I need to put some significance to the term "feminism" as I explore its changing meaning. For the purposes of this book, I will define feminism in the following way:

FEMINISM

Feminism represents views and teachings about women who take either a movement-oriented approach in which people form groups and caucuses on behalf of women, or an individual-oriented approach where a woman defines her own ideas about being a woman.

I do not think my definition of feminism is that rigid and it can not be because feminism is a collaboration of so many ideas about women. I will examine feminism from both the movement-oriented and individual-oriented approaches to assist you in understanding my definition of feminism.

FEMINISM
A MOVEMENT-ORIENTED APPROACH

If you ask people to define feminism you would probably get some responses like its the women's movement or women's lib. These are people who view feminism from the movement-oriented approach. The women's movement (or feminist movement as some call it) was a movement meant to address and draw attention to women's economic and political interests, women's social and gender relationships, women's health concerns, and a variety of issues that impact women. I feel the women's movement helped women become more organized and strengthened their impact by utilizing the media to bring exposure of women's issues to society. It was a time for women's voices to be heard and for them to verbalize and actively express their viewpoints about women's concerns.

There was a very formal and informal side to the women's movement. Many things were happening in the women's movement so the cause necessitated both a formal and informal structure. On the formal side, women were forming coalitions, caucuses, groups, and organizations. Officers were elected to organizations, feminist agendas were developed, and women spoke out to government officials about changing laws and developing new policies with women as the focus.

On a more informal level many women became involved and empowered by women's liberation gatherings and crowds. Women's liberation opened up dialogues for women by allowing them to discuss and network about feminist concerns. Women were able to gain awareness and support from one another for the common goal of spreading their message. The casual conversations at many of these women's rallies provided a place for women to give feed back to one another. These women became sources of strength for each other and empowered women to make changes in their lives.

As with any movement, one soon discovers that not everyone agrees or takes the same stand on the issues. This happened in the women's movement as women developed different interests and causes. Although many people today view the women's movement as one large distinctive movement, there are branches that move women in many directions.

Perhaps branching out in the women's movement gave women a chance to explore their causes more deeply. Early in the women's movement we heard about the women's suffrage movement as a campaign or crusade for the rights of women. In particular, women's suffrage leaders spoke out for women to have the right to vote. Later on, the women's movement branched out further. Some women concerned with domestic violence cultivated into battered women's type movements, and feminists concerned about pornography issues evolved into anti-pornography movements. Not all women agreed on the focus of the feminist issues. For instance, biblical feminists in a movement may be concerned with spiritual issues directly impacting their lifestyle, while equality feminists work on issues of pay equity in the workplace. The purposes and the agenda in the women's movement began to broaden as new issues surfaced.

FEMINISM
AN INDIVIDUAL-ORIENTED APPROACH

The other view of feminism is an individual-oriented approach where a woman defines her own ideas about being a woman. At first thought this approach bothered me. After all, if every woman defines feminism her own way, how can there be any consistency in the definition? Feminism would become so scattered there would be no clear direction for it to continue. As the years passed and I aged a little this individual-oriented approach did not bother me as much. In fact it seemed appealing to me. My ideas about feminism were evolving or changing and I seemed to be redefining feminism for myself. Even if women individually define feminism, there will be common ground and issues that surface over and over again.

Women will be redefining feminism as they go through life-cycle changes. Just as career interests change, family lifestyles change and the aging process occurs, women will be rethinking their views about feminism. Feminist concerns that were important in the early years of a woman's life may change as a woman ages and faces new obstacles. For example, a young, single feminist college student may not be interested in child care issues until she has children and a career to juggle. A young career feminist may not see the importance of the feminist issue of women's retirement benefits until she is older. Then her views begin to change and the issue becomes more pressing.

TYPES OF FEMINISTS

I have pondered hours about what feminism is or is not, but I wanted to know how other people felt about it. I asked several older people in a writing club to answer questions for me about their definition of feminism. The words that I constantly heard them use in their definitions were that it divided and separated women from men in a negative way. One person even commented that it was like saying, "I am woman," with an in-your-face kind of attitude. Their perspectives seemed to be that a failure of feminism was that it separated people and it did not adequately communicate the female perspective. I know these people each had their own ideas about feminism based on their education, family backgrounds and social experiences. They made the important point of being aware of how feminism is communicated to others. The message of what "feminism" is in our society is seen through many different eyes.

I asked a recent women's studies graduate about feminism one day. She promptly told me there were seven kinds of feminism. The graduate was very sure of her answer and left no room for discussion. Feminism has never been a term that I could define very quickly. It is not a term that I can write a definition for and feel complete about it. When I discuss feminism, I usually feel a need to explain myself. I want others to know how my feelings about feminism developed and changed over my life. My answers are not always simple about what is feminism. The reason for its complexity is based partly on the reaction I get from other people. Their misunderstandings cause me to have a yearning nature to explore new avenues and re-educate them about the broader picture of feminism and its meaning.

The question some people might ask a woman is, "Are you a feminist?" Somehow I never think they would be happy with a simple yes or no answer. For many people the word "feminist" is a loaded term that opens up the conversation to a national debate around the kitchen table. It triggers a hodgepodge of thoughts and ideas about women. Over the course of years, I have heard feminists being described in many different ways. I am not sure what all these types of feminists mean, but I am sure the idea of being a feminist can take many directions. One afternoon I started jotting down the classifications of feminists I had heard about in my life. It did not take long for me to realize that with such a diverse range of feminist thinking one could easily see why women had trouble agreeing on a definition of feminism. Books can be written describing the feminists' thinking related to these classifications. I certainly do not know what all these types of feminists entail, but I bet this is only a partial list of how feminists describe themselves.

The following words are descriptive tags that have been related to feminists:

1. Academic Feminists
2. Biblical Feminists
3. Contemporary Feminists
4. Cultural Feminists
5. Women of Color Feminists
6. Domestic Feminists
7. Radical Feminists
8. Historical Feminists
9. Career Feminists
10. Scholarly Feminists
11. Socialist Feminists
12. Marxist Feminists
13. Male Feminists
14. Reform Feminists
15. Pro Feminists
16. Equality Feminists

17.   Political Feminists

18.   Lesbian Feminists

19.   Liberal feminists

20.   Anti-porn Feminists

21.   Pro-Sex Feminists

22.   Young Feminists

23.   Intergenerational Feminists

24.   Ultra Feminists

25.   Collective Feminists

And the list goes on and on.

As you can see, feminists come in many forms. Are we expecting too much to think that all women could agree on a unified definition of feminism? My answer to that question is yes. There will always be some kind of controversy and disagreement over the issues of womanhood. As diverse as women are in their professions, their home-life and social roles, it seems impossible for all women to agree on a unified definition of feminism which encompasses so much. However, there may be bits and pieces of feminism that many women agree on whether they call it feminism or another label.

I am sure not everyone who reads this book will agree on all the things I have said about feminism. However, I have come to expect that in my years of writing, speaking and listening to women as we discuss the meaning of feminism. If understanding feminism was so easy it would not be challenging enough of us to continue our search for meaning. Listening to several heated discussions on feminism in casual conversations, and strong arguments on women's issues in academic circles, I started to notice one thing.

SEARCHING

Women are searching and exploring the meaning of feminism and trying to make sense of it. Some of my concerns about feminism have been actualized, while other women's issues are still ahead for me to explore. The purpose of this book is to search for the meaning of feminism by exploring some real life situations that have had an impact on my ideas about being a woman. This book will shed light and open doors on understanding both the feelings of resentment on feminism and the positive sources and strength women have gained from feminism. Women are at different stages in their search to find meaning in feminism. Numerous life events and career choices have made women meditate and deliberate past life decisions and future choices. Women ponder and search for answers to find a balance in their lives. The search for that balance often includes a re-examination of the ideas of being woman and the issues that are important in their personal lives. The search a woman takes to find and explore feminism comes at different times in the life cycle and is often related to the self-confidence of a woman.

CHAPTER TWO
FEMINISM AND LIFE CYCLE CHANGES

If you ask college women about their views on feminism you will get some very firm and strong answers. Some feel they have figured out feminism and know what they want in life at a young age. However, these young feminists are not aware of how life cycle changes have an impact on their feminist thinking. Life cycle changes such as a wedding and marriage, having a child, or losing a spouse may totally change one's feminist views.

I have heard the college freshman swear she will never become married and walk down the aisle. Several years later she wears a traditional wedding dress, walking down the church aisle and repeating the wedding vows like she swore she would never do. She may even find herself submitting to other things that contradict her personal feminist convictions. For example, she may feel strongly that women should have a voice in religious settings and in the decision making of a church. However, through her marriage she becomes involved in a church that does not allow her to express her views in that organized religious structure. As a result, the young feminist may experience internal conflict as her religious experience and feminist ideology do not mesh. In reality that is only one of the many internal conflicts a woman might face as life cycle changes occur.

I can honestly say that my feelings abut feminism and religion has changed throughout my life. As a young girl, I was raised in a Protestant religion where women had a voice and their opinions were valued. I married a young man who was actively involved in a very conservative religious group. For several years, I sat through church services and Bible lessons where women were highly criticized. Women were not allowed to take any leadership part of the church services and were criticized harshly about the length of their hair, their use of make-up, and the clothes they wore. It seemed that women were to be quiet, submissive and of course never criticize or question their husbands. My husband and I realized that this type of thinking did not mesh with our ideas and values.

We went through a phase where we no longer wanted to be part of an organized religious group. It was during this time that I really looked at my feminism and realized that I had repressed and held back ideas about religion because of the church structure. I put up with religious leaders who cut down the dignity of women as if it was the natural thing to do.

Years later, I joined a church again and it was the same Protestant religion that I had grown up in where women had a voice. I knew it was right for me as I saw women serving as ministers and lay readers during worship services. I saw women serving as deacons and elders and having a voice in the church and actively taking part in meeting together on a weekly basis. Being part of a religious group where I feel comfortable expressing my feminism and ideas about being a woman is an important part of my life. As my views about feminism change throughout my life cycle, it is comforting to know that I can express them freely through my religion.

I also found myself as a woman struggling with the area of freedom versus tradition in my life and religion. The church I attend is very casual about clothing. It is not uncommon for women to wear jeans, sweats or comfortable clothing to a church service. I know I have the freedom to wear whatever I choose to the church service, but I still find myself following back on tradition. I was raised in Oklahoma where people wore the "Sunday best" clothes to church. On Sunday morning, I am still putting on a dress to wear to church because it has been so ingrained in my thinking. I periodically wear jeans to church meetings or fellowship events, but I still struggle with the ideas of freedom and tradition when it comes to wearing a dress for the Sunday morning church service.

The issue of freedom verses tradition impacts a woman's daily choices. For example, a woman has the freedom to get up in the morning and go to work with out make-up, but she still traditionally wears it everyday to work. I also think about freedom and tradition with dating relationships. Women have the freedom to ask men out on dates, but some women still enjoy a man asking them out on dates. The choices women make are influenced by their family values, culture, psychological, social and economic conditions. It is the freedom to make these choices that is an exciting option for women. However, some women lack the self-confidence to know that they are given the freedom of choices.

Another area where young feminists deal with life cycle changes is in career development and its relationship to child bearing. For instance, some career oriented women have no interest in having children early in their professional careers. They are busy working on graduate degrees, career networking, committee memberships, and making their mark in a chosen career. I have heard young career women swear they would never have children or take care of a child. They may even go to great lengths regarding the topic of birth control. The birth control pill and other contraceptive methods may be used, but some career women feel so strongly about not having children that they get a tubal ligation. As some career oriented women become established in careers there is an increased desire to have children. It is not uncommon for career women who say they would never bear children to change their minds and have a child in their thirties and forties. Some of these women will have a tubal ligation reversal operation, go through in vitro fertilization or adopt children to meet the change of their desires.

In summation, life cycle changes have an impact on our feminist thinking. They cause us to rethink our priorities and our desires. We are not always prepared to understand how our feminist viewpoints shift twenty years later whether we call ourselves feminists or not. Each life event, career decision and personal choice influences how a woman feels about herself. As a woman ages she puts those life events and situations in perspective.

DIFFERENT PATHS

My sister Myral and I choose very different paths in life. Although, we were only one year apart in age our adult worlds seemed to be heading in totally opposite directions. Well, at least that's what I thought fifteen years ago. I now wonder if we want the same things in life but in a different order or pattern. Myral, my older sister was the shy daughter, who always did what she was told without question. I was the younger, more outspoken daughter who questioned the equality and fairness issues in our family.

Oddly enough, Myral and I both moved out of our parents home while we were in our teen age years. Myral married young and was expecting her first child in her late teens. Myral never pursued a career beyond high school and went on to produce a total of seven wonderful children. She had chosen the path of homemaker and a stay at-home mom. Her husband had a good job and she seemed content for the most part of the lifestyle that she had chosen.

I on the other hand moved out of my parents' house at age sixteen and was determined to complete my college degrees and start a career. I had the career feminist idea that career was everything and having babies was a secondary role that could be delayed for many years or that didn't have to occur at all. I had my doctoral degree by age twenty-three and taught college and elementary school in my mid twenties. I worked hard in my career path winning several national awards and becoming an associate professor by the age of thirty. I was fairly content and thought I had life figured out, but then my desires and priorities began to change.

My sister and I rarely saw each other over the next fifteen to twenty years except for an occasional family holiday once a year or a telephone call to catch up on family news. Geographically, we were miles apart over those years. She had moved several times for her husband's work relocation and I had been promoted and jostled around to several states for my university jobs.

I remember Myral calling me in my late thirties to invite me to her oldest son's high school graduation. I was busy writing and it had been a hectic afternoon for me so the timing of the phone call was inconvenient. However, it was clear that Myral really wanted to talk to me that afternoon and get some things off her chest. As I listened I was amazed at the nature and direction of her conversation which seemed almost totally reversed from the talks we had in our early years.

There was Myral, the quiet sister, who had chosen the path of the homemaker no longer sounding shy and opening up to me all her hopes and desires. Myral was now pondering whether to get an education and try to get a good job in case something happened to her husband. Myral had suddenly realized that she hardly had any retirement benefits because she had not worked outside the home. She shared with me her desire to travel and go on a cruise when her last child graduated from high school. This was a Myral that was ripe and ready to explore the world outside the home. Had all of these ideas and feelings been stored inside of her for years? Suddenly Myral was vocalizing some of those feminists' ideas that I so openly expressed fifteen years earlier. She never mentioned the word feminist in our conversation, but all the overtones were there.

I remember how Myral and I talked about what we would do if our husbands died. My response after fifteen years of marriage in an egalitarian dual career marriage was, "Sure, I would remarry again because marriage is terrific." Her response was quite different from mine. Myral's husband had always been strong willed and liked his family to operate according to his rules and demands. Myral responded that she would not want to be married again. Of course I would always give her room to change her mind. Perhaps, I was more stunned by the reason Myral gave for not wanting to remarry. Myral said she did not want to remarry because she wanted her independence. Myral desired the freedom to do all those things she had wanted to do for years. I had never heard Myral talk about independence before. Independence was a word I often used in my late teens and early twenties and yet Myral was almost forty years old before this type of feminist thinking was verbalized and she could see a light at the end of the tunnel.

ARE WE SO DIFFERENT?

I laughed to myself as I heard Myral say these things because I had already been through the path she was talking about on the phone. I had finished my degrees and had worked my way up the college teaching ladder. I had traveled around the country writing and presenting papers at professional conferences. I had enjoyed a wonderful childless dual career marriage with a supportive husband. I seemed to have it all in Myral's eyes.

Yet, by my late thirties, I started to desire that which I did not have. I did so many career things that I had begun to wonder about having a baby and settling down a little to raise a beautiful child. It is ironic that I savor the things my sister Myral has with her children and family and now she wants a taste of the career path I have experienced. After fifteen years of marriage and a family, Myral sounded more like a feminist and I sounded more like a homebody.

I began to ask myself if Myral and I shared similar views about feminism. Could it be that we just developed an appreciation for feminist ideas at different times throughout our life cycles? Could life events occurring throughout the life cycle effect our feelings and decisions about feminism? Perhaps Myral and I desired the same things, but we looked through different looking glasses to find them. The careers and families we desired were on different time lines. I wanted the career early and the family later, while Myral decided the family early and career ambitions later in life. Our life cycle experiences were different and that may have been why are ideas about feminism were developed differently.

LIFE CYCLE CHALLENGES

I believe that events occurring throughout a woman's life cycle can influence and change her views about feminism. The following is a list of some life cycle challenges that may shape or modify a woman's view of feminism:

*A woman's feelings about her career development and occupational choices

*Socialization experiences from elementary to high school

*Choice of a mate and/or marriage experiences

*Timing and choices related to parenthood

*Feelings and concerns about financial issues that impact a women and her family

*Family health concerns such as a sick or handicapped child

*Family social problems such as domestic violence or alcoholism

*Life goals change to new directions

*Loss of a family member

*Internal conflicts that are dealt with over a long period of time

*Education, counseling and human relations training that may cause a woman to look at her situation in a different way

*Influence from peers, mentors and family members

THE ROLES OF WOMEN

One reason that many women may be confused about feminism is that they define it by the roles they have in their lives. These different roles cause women to view their ideas of womanhood in a variety of ways. It gets even more confusing when women judge other women by the roles they have chosen in their lives. Take for example a woman who stays at home to raise her children and helps her husband in their family business. She feels positive about her lifestyle choice. The woman takes the children to school, volunteers for a class party, and carry her cellular phone if she needs to make a business call. Yet at times she feels those career women who work outside of the home look down on her as if what she does is not important. This woman feels she has made a healthy lifestyle choice that benefits not only her, but also her husband and children. She senses that other women see her as a housewife with a narrow focus and that they do not fully understand her role as a woman and her choices.

The following is a list of some of the varied roles that women undertake in our society:

*single, career woman

*woman in a dual career marriage

*woman working in home business

*woman choosing to stay at home with children

*woman in a care-taking role for sick husband or child

*woman taking a leave-of-absence from a career for family responsibilities or career growth

*woman experiencing a career change due to job restructuring or lay-off

*woman returning to school for additional education

*woman financially supporting spouse for future education

*woman making a move or relocation for her career or her spouse's career

*woman living apart from spouse and family with a job in a separate location and having to commute by plane or car

*working woman with a stay-at-home spouse

*working woman with an extended family

*single parent working woman

*woman in high profile career

This list of roles for women can go on and on, but there are other factors one must consider to understand the scenario of feminism. One such factor is that of change. A stay-at-home mom decides to get an education or take a job and her role changes. Her societal role has changed and so has her perspectives and insights on feminism. Issues that did not concern her when she stayed at home with her children now become real challenges. Suddenly, she may become concerned about salary, flex-time, costs and quality of day care and sharing household duties with her spouse. The woman's role has changed and new horizons have opened up in her life. She is not sure that other women really understand her stress, the complexities of her situation and what she is going through. The woman will probably discover along the way that she does have common problems and concerns with other women who have had similar experiences, even if her situation seems unique.

As the woman's roles change they have an impact on other family members. For instance, take a woman with a young child who decides to return to college. She needs to take a Monday night class and her husband has to baby-sit. He becomes frustrated because he has to give up his Monday night football with his buddies. Because her role has changed, her husband's house hold role has also changed and now new male and female communication issues arise.

Issues related to role changes have developed for many years as women have made decisions to go to college and get an education. I have heard "war stories" of husbands who refuse to pay tuition, refuse to attend their wife's college graduation, and are non-supportive of the idea of a woman receiving an education to better herself. I met a college professor whose spouse absolutely did not want her to attend college so he would hide her car keys. Years later some men will change and become more accepting of women working, especially when they see the earning potential and how it can improve their lifestyle.

In trying to understand feminism one can picture an array of women in a number of roles that are constantly changing. If a group of women are discussing feminist issues, often one of them will have a disagreement, difference of opinion, or a misunderstanding. The reason this occurs is because women are at different levels of understanding regarding changes in their life. There are many life cycle challenges that cause a woman to rethink her views and modify her feelings about feminism. For some women ideas and thoughts about feminism are clear-cut and direct. I feel there are other women who go through a life style change and as a result form new views on feminism. Life events, family circumstances and job situations can greatly influence how a woman sees herself.

CHAPTER THREE
FEMINISM
AND THE DUAL CAREER MARRIAGE

COLLEGE YEARS

For many young women, college is a focal point for learning about feminism and independence. It was exciting for me because I was one of those early entry students. I had skipped my senior year at high school and at the age of sixteen I was a full time college student living in the dorm several hours from my home town.

I loved attending a small liberal arts campus and opening my mind up to all the different points of view. A sociology major with a communications minor seemed like the logical direction for me. Class discussions were great and I soon learned there were other women voicing their concerns on the issue of equality. I savored the independence of being my own person and doing my own thing the first few years of college. Love and marriage were no where in my focal point so enjoying the aspects of the feminist lifestyle seemed natural.

OOPS, THE FEMINIST FELL IN LOVE

Of course I do not remember any of my classes discussing feminism as part of love and marriage. College dating was a good experience for me in discovering my feminism. I quickly learned there were some men I could not possibly fall in love with or marry. By my senior year love had stepped into the picture and I had begun to change some of my hard-core feminist beliefs that all men were difficult and unfair to women. I met a young man named Alan who as a young college student himself, listened to my ideas and accepted me with my ideas about feminism. The strong-willed, determined feminist was getting a soft heart and falling into the life cycle stage of love and marriage.

PERSONALITY PROFILES

Becoming engaged at the tender age of twenty-one was scary for a feminist like me. Was I going to give up all the independence I loved so much by getting married and being in a "submissive type" of relationship? How could I give up my nontraditional feminist thinking and be married in a traditional wedding ceremony as my parents had done so many years ago?

To combat some of our misgivings my fiancee and I went through premarital counseling. Of course, the first thing the counselor asked us to do was to take personality profiles so that we could understand each other's personality a little better. The results of the personality profile were not surprising in the least. The counselor pointed out that I (the female in the relationship) scored very high in the area of dominance, which meant I liked to control and dominate things. My fiancee scored much lower in the area of dominance and was downright submissive and too agreeable. The counselor's suggestion was that I should not try to dominate so much and that my future husband should become more aggressive in the relationship.

Years later in examining our personality types, we realized that we had both changed. There were times we both had to give in and forgive to make the marriage work. Issues that were so pressing and important in the early years of marriage changed after the college years were over and the relationship reached new stages of our career development.

CHANGING MY NAME

There I was walking down the church aisle in that long white wedding dress. I almost fell on my face as I realized I had never worn a dress like this before and it was way too difficult to move in my usual manner. This was very different from the jeans and cowhand boots I wore in high school. What was I getting myself into with this marriage business?

I can not believe I changed my name and started going by my husband's name which was something I swore I would never do. Although, this name change thing bothered me some, I found I went through more than one actual name change. I am not so sure that I changed my name strictly for feminist reasons.

The first few years of marriage I used my hyphenated maiden and married name. I was content because I still had my single identity and my married identity. Several years down the road I was tired of using both names. No one ever spelled or pronounced my difficult maiden name correctly, and I was tired of writing the fifteen-letter hyphenated name on a grocery store check every-week. So, I dropped using the maiden name in my professional and personal life.

Well, I started using my married name Susan Peterson and that was easy to spell and pronounce. The only problem was that my name was not unique and everywhere I moved I met numerous women with the my same name. So I have decided to include my middle name and address myself as Susan Louise Peterson. As a young college student with feminist ideas, I never knew all the elements that could influence a name change.

The name change seemed like such a big issue early in the marriage, but its relative importance dwindled quickly as other marriage issues surmounted. I may have changed my name, but my feminist ways were still very strong in establishing and forming the marital relationship.

BABY BLUES

There were some scary moments in the early years of marriage that put my feminist lifestyle in jeopardy. I remember walking across the college campus after a trip to the campus medical center. The doctor was running a pregnancy test and my young husband and I looked into each other's eyes with the shock that we might be parents. We just were not ready for the idea of having a baby so early in our marriage. We were a future dual career couple and getting our degrees seemed the most important thing. With college loans stacking up and our savings shrinking quickly, a baby was just not in the picture.

My mind raced as I contemplated how I could write a doctoral dissertation and survive comps with a baby. My career meant everything to me and the idea of having an unplanned baby was a scary proposition. Luckily, the test results showed that I was not pregnant and it was just a missed period. My husband and I have not forgotten that scary moment early in our marriage.

I remember how I was absolutely against having children when I was a young, married college student in my mid twenties. Part of this attitude about children was related to the culture and community where I was raised. I came from a large family. We lived in an agricultural setting. The ideas from years ago were that a family had many children to help on the farm and do the chores. With today's modern farm equipment, a family really does not need twelve kids to feed the livestock. There were several other families in my community that had large families. I was raised hearing remarks like, "She is pregnant again," and, "They do not have enough money to raise a baby," and, "Why do they need another child?," and, "She is the last person who needs to be having a baby," and so on. After hearing these comments, I feel I started associating pregnancy and having babies as a negative thing that ruined your life.

In my feminist mind, I related pregnancy and childbirth as an interference to my career goals. I connected having children as an interruption of my career plans and as something that would put my marriage in debt. It was not until I had earned my college education and paid off my student loans and become well established in a professional career that I began to have an interest and desire to have children.

An interest and desire to bear a child is not the same for all women. It develops at different times and in different ways. Some women are content with a experiencing a childless lifestyle while others may nurture the desire to have a baby later in life. There are women who have children in their teens and then have their tubes tied. Later in life they experienced a desire to have more children. A woman's interest and desire to have a child is a very personal decision which is influenced by one's life cycle, family relationship, career plans and a number of other factors in her life. Women who have chosen the career path and delayed child bearing for years may face expensive medical treatments and difficulty in having children in mid life. While career goals have dominated their thoughts early in life, a baby may become the one thing to fulfill the dream of "having it all" for these women.

WEDDING RING SYNDROME

I remember early in my marriage when I always wore my wedding ring and of course I expected my husband to wear his ring. It was like a security blanket to represent our wedding vows and the sanctity of our marriage. Well, I lost my wedding ring during the first year of our marriage. I bought another wedding band and I lost it a few years later. Finally, after a few more lost wedding rings, I began to wear wedding bands less frequently. My husband was actually very good about wearing his wedding band and he did not lose it for fifteen years.

We had a strong and stable marriage and neither of us were wearing wedding rings. I believe a wedding ring is a beautiful symbol of a relationship and its importance dwindles as issues of commitment and respect become prominent. Traditional symbols such as wedding rings are attractive but for many women with feminist beliefs the ideas of respect, appreciation of each other's ideas, and a mutual understanding of a marriage partner or spouse is a much greater gift.

HOUSEHOLD DUTIES

Coming from a family where males did not help with housework, I did not know what to expect in my dual career marriage. I was lucky in my marriage because many of the household duties were completed together. My husband and I made many trips to the laundry mat to wash and dry multiple loads of clothes. We found we each had talents so our household duties were divided by what we liked to do and what we did well. I liked to cook so I cooked and he was excellent at washing the dishes so cleaning the kitchen became his job. Later on as our careers developed, a housekeeper service became inevitable as neither of us had much time for household duties. My negative childhood experience about males helping with household duties was not the issue I thought it would be in marriage. I had married a man who was willing to help with chores and do his equal share of work around the house. I know that for some women this is a much bigger issue which requires discussion about household expectations from both partners.

WHAT ABOUT THE MONEY?

What started out as a simple financial plan in early marriage became a little more complicated for this dual career marriage. Our first jobs out of college were as teachers in the public schools. The salaries were exactly the same so dividing the income was relatively easy. We simply had three accounts. My spouse and I deposited our paychecks in separates accounts. We then opened a general account and put an equal amount of money in the account to pay bills. This worked fine for a while as long as our incomes were the same.

Because of my ambitious nature I started an aggressively climb the career ladder. The following ten years meant frequent moves and variations in pay salaries as I moved from being a school teacher through a series of jobs up to an Associate Professor. I started making ten thousand dollars more a year than my husband. Putting our paychecks in our accounts was not working so well anymore. We decided to put both paychecks into a general account and then give each other an equal allowance to save, spend or blow as we chose. This worked better for equality in the dual career marriage. Our money management patterns changed by the salaries we made and the positions we held at various times throughout the marriage. Through fifteen years of marriage our family money management system was adjusted periodically. As long as the issue of fairness was respected by both spouses, the accounting system could change numerous times in our marriage.

RELOCATION

I never really thought about job relocation as a feminist issue until I viewed it in a dual career marriage situation. After all, teaching college was not the easiest field to find an abundance of jobs. Job offers to a beginning professor were few and were often in remote locations. I was determined to move up the career ladder quickly even if it meant moving to some small town every couple of years.

During a ten year period my husband and I lived in apartments and kept few possessions so that we could move quickly if a better job offer came my way. He was supportive of the money I spent copying and mailing out hundreds of resumes. The job offers were few, but every couple of years I would get a position slightly better than the one I had and we would pack up the truck and move on down the road. For ten years my husband moved willingly as I purged ahead with my career. Luckily, at each place we lived he was able to obtain a teaching position in the public schools. During these many years he put his career second to mine, and he probably gave up a few career advancements for himself so that I could succeed in my career.

WHAT IF THE TABLES WERE TURNED

Some people would say I had had the perfect dual-career marriage for my career feminist ideas. I wonder how they would view it if the tables were turned? What if I decided to put my career on hold so that I could help my husband move up the career ladder? What if I decided to take a career break and raise children for a few years while he puts more energy into his career development? Would I still be viewed as a feminist? Am I only a feminist if it benefits my career and my husband supports my career? If I chose to support my husband's career over my career am I less of a feminist? These questions are real and pragmatic in present dual career marriages. Researchers have many opportunities to investigate the views and feelings about feminism in the dual career marriage setting. When dual career spouses make sacrifices and adjustments for each other's career, how is it viewed in terms of feminist thinking? Does feminism only support the choice a woman makes if it is beneficial to her career? Are career decisions that benefit the husband's career seen as less important in the eyes of feminists?

CHAPTER FOUR
FEMINISM AND ANGER

One concern I have always had about writing and discussing feminism was the anger connected with it. I have seen anger come from both men and women over the issue of women. I remember my college days as I sat in a Women's Studies seminar. I thought it would be enjoyable and enlighten my feminist views. It was not long before the discussion turned ugly and the anger appeared. Female students started expressing their anger and hatred toward men. I thought to myself, "Wait a minute, I like men." I wanted to appreciate the aspects of being a woman without degrading the opposite sex. I think social situations influence my viewpoints on feminism. When I was around a group of women who were angry and hated men, I would say, "I am not an angry feminist." Yet when a dinner discussion of the topic of equal pay for equal work came up, I did not hesitate to talk about the issues of equality and fairness.

The anger of feminism was not always directed toward the opposite sex. I observed angry encounters from women toward each other when they discussed feminist issues. The emotions would flare up between two women with opposing viewpoints. The conversation would usually end with a hatred between the women. The issue was not usually resolved because of harsh viewpoints and lost respect for each other. Over the years I have tried to analyze where this anger comes from when discussing feminist issues and women's studies. The following are some of the reasons I think women and men argue about feminism and women's issues:

LACK OF KNOWLEDGE

Some of the arguments surrounding feminism come because people have a lack of knowledge about the subject. I was sitting in a restaurant once with my husband when he told the waitress I was a writer. When I told her that I was writing a women's studies book, she became angry. She argued that she had read a feminist book and it was clearly a demise to all women for the topic of women's studies to be discussed. Her view of feminism was apparently shaped by one book she had read.

Often a person will read a magazine article, watch a television program or listen to a church service, and be so influenced by one viewpoint that he or she considers him or her self an expert on issues of feminism. Once these people are around other people that question their viewpoints and raise new issues they become offended and angry. I have studied women and feminist issues for years. I am always learning new things and ideas that cause me to ask new questions and search for new sources of understanding. In difficult and angry discussions about feminism it is good to make helpful suggestions for further reading that can enhance a person's knowledge and see the broader picture of feminism. Some women do not seek to learn about feminism until they face job or life issues that impact their self dignity. A woman who has experienced sexual harassment or employment discrimination may start researching feminism to understand particular issues that effect her lifestyle. The urge to learn about feminism often comes from a woman's desire to be treated fairly and to have an inner peace.

DIFFERENT STAGES IN THE LIFECYCLE

Another reason for anger in feminist discussions is that people are at different stages in their life cycles and do not always express their views in the same format. One person may have worked through a feminist situation successfully, while another in the class has never dealt with the issue. A person who has never had a child may not understand the issues surrounding the issue of child-care that a dual career parent faces. These different stages of the life cycle put people in different levels of understanding and at different emotional states. We probably notice differences as a matter of personality, but often they are closely tied to evolving life cycles stages.

WOMEN'S LACK OF SUPPORT FOR EACH OTHER

I was a very young graduate student and I guess I was very naive about the working world. I had survived the dissertation trauma and with absolutely no work experience I had my doctorate at twenty-three, but no job. The first step after college was getting a job. Was I worried? No, because all I had to do was what my college professors had told me to do. Their advice was pretty simple. First I needed a woman to mentor me and show me the ropes. Second, I needed to network through women's clubs and organizations. I figured if I did these two things I would have no problem finding a job in six months before my college loans caught up with me.

As I think about their advice years later, neither of their suggestions helped me get a job. First, I never met a woman who wanted to take on the task of being my mentor. A few women professors wrote letters of recommendations for my placement file, but that was the extent of their help. In fact from all my college years, I can think of only one professor who helped mentor me and he was a male communications professor who made me rewrite my papers three or four times to assist me in improving my writing skills. Most of the women I knew were too busy working toward their own career goals.

I do not mean to sound negative but the lack of support I have seen between women has been minimal. I really did not think about it much until I received a survey full of questions about how college women have mentored and helped me after graduation. I started to fill out the survey, but I became so discouraged thinking about the lack of support from mentoring that I threw it away in disgust.

I tried my professors second piece of advice and that was networking through clubs and organizations. I joined women's clubs and organizations confident they would help me move up the career ladder. I found that some of the organizations did not exactly share my philosophies about women. This advice did not help either and when the college loans came due, I had run out of money to pay the club dues.

I finally reached my career goals, but unfortunately it was on my own and without a woman mentor or network group supporting me. I simply did it the old fashion way by hard work. I mailed out resumes and transcripts and made hundreds of telephone calls. I started at the low paying jobs and worked up the levels of teacher, instructor, assistant professor and associate professors. I have made career changes since then, but it has been because I have gone through periods of change and re-evaluation of my career goals.

I still think about the women who feel anger and pain from the lack of support they receive from other women. From my personal experiences I can empathize and understand their frustration and anger. I believe a young woman's frustration may change as she grows older and has more positive experiences with other women. She may develop skills later in her career that enable her to work more effectively with mentors and organizations that she lacked in the early career years. Even though a woman does not have positive mentoring experiences herself, it does not stop her from becoming a mentor to other women.

INTERDISCIPLINARY DISAGREEMENTS

Some academia department may not may not fully agree with ideas about women. Many Women's Studies programs are interdisciplinary in nature. The positive side of this is that it brings many points of view to women's studies and opens the door for many discussions and questions. The negative side of being an interdisciplinary type of program is that some of the departments on campus may not fully appreciate the aspects of feminism and women's issues as the faculty do. As a result, some students and faculty may get angry and challenge the outside department on their views about feminism. Some of these problems can be avoided by having the women's studies department fully explain the depth and breadth of the program to faculty members in other academic fields.

SINGLE ISSUE FOCUS

Some women seem angry about feminism based on a single issue focus. They may disagree with one single aspect of feminism which causes them to bring anger at the entire feminist view. A good example of this would be a woman who does not support feminism because she feels strongly against birth control based on her religious beliefs. As a woman I can respect her personal choice related to her body, her reproductive alternatives, and birth control preferences. However a woman does not have to turn her back on all elements of feminism that have helped her and will help her future children to have a better life. She may be enjoying better pay, more benefits or extended family leave based on laws that feminist developed and contributed to society. However, she bases her anger and dislike about feminism on a single issue instead of the broader picture.

Anger about feminism will not end overnight. As long as people are frustrated about feminist issues in their lives, there will be angry conflicts. By seeking to understand why people get angry about feminism we can at least find ways to help them. If they have a lack of knowledge about feminism we can try to educate them. As they go through life cycle stages we can seek to understand their emotional levels. If they are angry at the lack of support from other women, then we can provide them with support and encouragement. If faculty from other departments lack understanding about women's issues then we can explain new ideas and program goals. These strategies will not end anger toward the subject of feminism, but may help women and men improve communication between each so the topic can be discussed in academic and social settings with greater understanding.

CHAPTER FIVE
THE LITTLE THINGS ABOUT FEMINISM

In my quest for meaning in feminism I found there were some little things about feminism that pinched me in the side. There were many matters that still frustrated me a little. Some feminists may not share my perspective on these little things and that's okay. For other feminists I hope to provide information on little things about feminism and open a door to a different perspective.

WORDS AND FEMINISM

When I first started studying about feminism years ago, the emphasis was on words. How were women addressed and what labels were used to describe them? If men referred to woman as girls, do we choose to correct them and clarify their statement with a feminist speech that we are women and not girls. If someone referred to a woman as a mailman, did we quickly responded she is a mail carrier? Women made a big issue about sexist language and phrases that were supposedly prejudiced against women. I may have been guilty of harshly correcting someone who used an inappropriate phrase to address me as a woman.

However over the years I have made a human relations type observation of what I see happening when a feminists make a big issue over how they are addressed. I will use my friend Sally as an example. Sally was a single professional woman in her mid thirties who befriended my husband and I. She would call us and come over to dinner several nights a week and Sally shared many of my feminist ideas over the months of our friendship. On a particular occasion one of our male friends named Carl stopped over for dinner and conversation with Sally and us. The dinner conversation was great until we were about to leave for a movie and Carl said "Let's get going, girls." Sally immediately attacked Carl for referring to women as girls. I noticed something happening in the communication during the rest of the evening. The communication between Sally and Carl ceased that evening. The way Carl had addressed the women as girls, whether it was intentional or unintentional, became the overriding issue of the night and all other topics in the conversation were put to rest.

I think about how many times I have heard feminists say "the good ole boy's network." So I wonder what women will say if they hear men refer to them as "the good ole girl's network"? Are women going to correct them and say it is the "good ole woman's network"? Can a woman criticize a man for calling her a girl if she refers to herself that way. In Oklahoma I have heard many men refer to themselves as being an "Oklahoma boy". I may have been guilty a few times of referring to myself as an "Oklahoma girl." If I have referred to myself as a girl, then how can I become angry at a man who makes the same comment. For some women the overriding issue that impacts their responses is not what they are called, but rather what social context is it used.

In my professional working life I meet men everyday. I have a choice in how I respond to them regarding the way they address me. I am different from Sally in that I usually do not make an issue of it unless I find it is totally offensive, degrading and derogatory to me as a woman. If I am in a professional setting with a man who respects my career just as I respect his career, I want to maintain a positive working relationship. If we are working and collaborating on a long term project everyday I am not going to make a big issue over whether he referred to me as a woman or a girl in casual conversation. The reason I do not want to make such a big issue about it is partly because I want to leave the doors open for further communication so I can learn more about him and the project. I prefer not to ruin a positive working relationship with a man by going overboard on one small word or phrase from the many thousands of words a person uses in a day.

The person sending the message may be using a verbal tone or facial expression that causes a woman to become angry with how she is addressed. A man shouting at a woman and saying, "Get yourself over here girl," is sending a message that will easily anger many women. On the other hand, a husband who lovingly tells his wife that she is, "His favorite girl," will probably get a different response. In different social situations women might react in a variety of ways. They respond to a person who is sending a message in a particular the social setting, and women may react according to the events that are happening now or earlier that day. There are many factors that might influence a woman's reaction to a particular phrase or statement about women.

Perhaps the differences between feminists over sexist language are what one woman finds offensive, derogatory or degrading, may not bother another woman at all. I know there are men and women who say extremely degrading things toward women and I usually choose not be around most of them. In some situations I try to educate or redirect the person making the derogatory statement, and to reason a different view toward women. When women desire to correct a person on an issue related to words or sexist language, they need to stop before they make a direct attack on the individual making the statement. Feminists need to have a sensitivity to that person's educational and emotional level. They need to think about the type of relationship they want with the person making the sexist remark. Most importantly feminist must determine if the remark was meant to be truly derogatory, degrading or offensive, or was just a light hearted remark.

The following is a strategy for redirecting sexist language without making the person who made the sexist remark feel degraded or foolish. The old strategy many women used carried a negative overtone. For example a person makes the statement, "Oh, you are a mailman?"

Old Strategy Feminist Response

"I am not a mailman, but I am a mail carrier."

In this response there is the negative statement of using the word no and then correcting the person. I propose a new strategy for dealing with sexist remarks. It is not new because educators have been using this approach with children for years. The new strategy is simply to respond to the person making the sexist statement by saying the correct feminist term back without a negative tone. Two examples are given below:

Sexist Remark: "Oh, you are a mailman."
New Strategy Response: "Yes, I deliver mail in my job as a mail carrier."

Sexist Type Remark: "Oh, how long have you been a salesman?"
New Strategy Response: "I have been a salesperson for five years."

FEMINISM AND EQUALITY

Early on with my feminist way of thinking I had the idea that everything that related to feminism had to be so in terms of equality. I felt everything should be equal when it came to the sexes. I guess you can say I was an equality feminist. I still can not get out of my mind the idea of equal pay for equal work that has been around for years. Let me however give an example of something regarding feminism and equality that has bothered me for years.

I am sure that many women have had experiences related to the size of women's restrooms in churches and public places. I know this sounds like a silly example, but bare with me. When a blueprint of a church is developed and the building committee puts three stalls in the men's restroom and three stalls in the women's restroom, should the feminists applaud the keen insight of the architect and building committee for placing an equal number of stalls in each restroom? It might look good on paper until the practicality of the restroom is addressed.

I was visiting a new church building in a big metropolitan city, while on a vacation. The restroom situation really bothered me that day. Outside of the men's restroom were no waiting lines and or hassles to get inside. The women's restroom was a different story. I waited almost an hour in a long line to go into one of the three bathroom stalls. It was apparent from a practical standpoint that there needed to be more stalls in the women's restroom. Three stalls seemed to be efficient in meeting the needs of the males in the congregation, but three stalls did not address the female restroom needs. The issue was not on having an equal number of restrooms for both sexes, but on whether women should be involved in the planning. I do not know if there has been research on the amount of time males and females spend in the restroom, but a person does not have to be a research scientist to observe the problem with the modern restroom.

Perhaps, the problem was not really about the equal number of restrooms for males and females in the church. The problem probably was that women were not given a voice in regards to the blueprints and planning of the new church building. If women's advice is given consideration, then the needs and concerns of women should be addressed and the problem of long lines outside the church restroom should be avoided.

MEN-ARE THEY THE ENEMY?

For years the topics important to women have been studied in various university departments. In the present time we are seeing an interest in men's studies in programs, courses, seminars and groups. Are these programs a threat to women's studies? No, of course not, I applaud men for seeking a better understanding of their needs, goals and values. There is a wonderful opportunity for women's studies faculty to collaborate with researchers in the field of men's studies. Research projects dealing with the issues of male and female relationships, workplace behavior, and dual career marriages are just a few of the projects that could be conducted and intermingled between these two departments.

As a young girl raised in rural Oklahoma, I thought boys were the enemy. It probably came from my family background of having five brothers. I was what people called a "tomboy" growing up in the country. I guess in a way I really wanted to be like the boys as a young girl because boys in my family did not have to clean house or cook. Boys could stay out as late as they wanted and the family rules were very flexible for boys while the girls had many rules and strict guidelines. I so admired the freedoms of the boys in my young years that I did not think it would be much fun to become a woman. I enjoyed wearing cowboy, or is it cowgirl boots?, and blue jeans all through junior high and high school along with the dress my mother made me wear to church on Sundays.

During my teenage and college years I totally changed my view. I really began to love myself as being a "woman" and could appreciate men without wanting to act or dress like a man. I began to see some wonderful relationships where women and men complimented each other and had positive working and marital relationships. The boys I once saw as enemies, had become men that I collaborated with in my accomplishments.

WHO RAISED YOU?

Beliefs about feminism are also influenced by the family structure. A person raised in a single parent family may not view home and work responsibilities for women the same way as someone raised with two parents. The task and duties projected by parents to children differ according to who raised the children. If boys and girls are expected to share in the household duties, the children will have different perspectives about feminism than a family that only expects girls to do the housework. These early family influences have a powerful effect on how adults perceive the roles of the sexes throughout the life cycle.

PORTRAYAL OF WOMEN

On occasion when I watch television, I have noticed how women are portrayed. I think about the show, "The Beauty and the Beast," and how the sensitive woman finds strength in the beast no matter how he looks. I would love to see a version of that show with a woman as the beast and a sweet sensitive man responding with great kindness to her.

I have a friend who constantly reads romance novels and has probably read a thousand novels. She once told me that of all the novels she has read she only remembers one where the man falls in love with a very plain, ordinary looking woman and the book's focus was on the inner beauty of the woman. Her observation was that most romance novels still focused around the portrayal of beautiful women based on their looks and physical beauty.

I think it even goes further when one looks at commercials and advertisements about skin care products. It almost seems as if our society treats sun screen as a woman's product. I know women who wear sunscreen lotions for daily sun protection. I live in Las Vegas, Nevada where the sun is extreme and harsh on the skin. I drive by construction housing sites where most men do not wear sun screen and most take off their shirts when temperatures climb into the hundreds. I wonder if men think that taking care of skin is something that women do and that they are immune from skin cancer. I have rarely seen my husband of fifteen years of marriage put on sunscreen. He has put on sunscreen once or twice for a vacation, but sees no need to wear it on a daily basis. Has society portrayed the use of skin care products as a woman's only concern?

SLOW CHANGING EXPECTATIONS

Feminists see the changes that society has made and is making, but some people are slow to change their expectations in our fast paced society. I remember taking a home economics course in junior high school and I could not get the hang of sewing. On the very last day of school after all of the other students had left, my teacher made me stay and tear out and replace the hem of the blouse. I was so frustrated that when my mother picked me up at five o'clock, I broke into tears. My mother swore to me that I would never have to take a home economics class again.

Little did I know that years later when I decided to pursue my doctoral degree in family relations and child development, it would be housed in (you guessed it) the school of home economics. My other college degrees were in sociology and human relations, so I was used to expressing my opinions freely and having my viewpoint heard and accepted. The field of home economics was a little different. Sure, I heard people talking about dual career marriages and writing about them, but there was an undertone of not saying too much or being caught with your foot in your mouth.

I noticed this even more when I was a faculty member in a home economics department. I have never cooked, cleaned and done as many dishes in any other professional job as when I was college professor in a small home economics department. Every student reception, faculty event or informal meeting had to be prepared meticulously and to perfection. As a young, dual career marriage professional, I was also busy writing journal articles and trying to move up the career ladder. I soon realized that cooking and food preparation was taking hours of my time, so I thought I would make a few helpful suggestions that would save time and help me to enjoy my dual career marriage at home.

My relatively simple suggestions and ideas were shot down immediately. The department expectations were that all hors d'oeuvres had to be hand made and this took virtually hours. I suggested that I could run to the grocery store and pick up a loaf of bread or a bag of dinner rolls to go with the meal. I was quickly corrected that we would only serve homemade bread and rolls. We were virtually spending hours washing the dishes and cleaning up after these events. I haphazardly suggested that at the next event we should use paper plates. I was told immediately that this home economics department would never stoop so low as to use paper plates, even for a small informal reception. Luckily, not all home economics departments are like the one I worked in. I would add that home economics does a lot of research on women's issues in the areas of consumer and family studies.

I quickly learned that this was not a place I could work. There I was, standing before college students and teaching young women to express their ideas, to be themselves and enjoy the freedoms of life. Yet, I was working in a professional setting that hampered my freedom to express myself as I was striving to be an independent and successful career woman. There are some places in our society where expectations are slow to change. Despite the steps to move ahead and have a new vision for women, there are still obstacles that women painfully address each day in work and home situations.

CHAPTER SIX
CAREER FEMINISM AND NEGATIVITY

A woman choosing the career path must deal with her feminism in relationship to any negativity. I hate to say it, but negative remarks abound in the workplace and job related environments. While most women want to stay upbeat about their careers, they are faced with an array of negative remarks that discourage them and cause them to have doubts about their potential. Even the slightest remark may have a demeaning effect on a career feminist and cause her to lose focus of her goals. The key is turning these negative remarks into positive feminist career experiences.

YOU'LL NEVER DO THAT

Sometimes when a career feminist tells a person one of her ideas she will get a very negative remark that could totally discourage her from doing the thing she had set out to do. I remember telling a female colleague that I wanted to apply for jobs so that I could be promoted from an assistant professor to an associate professor. Her response was "You will never do that and if you did it will take you seven to ten years to achieve that goal." That negative attitude made me want to work twice as hard to prove her wrong. I applied for college teaching jobs and within six months I had been offered a job as associate professor. I had a choice of what I did with that negative remark. I could have taken her negative advice and stopped trying for the job promotion or work twice as hard to make a positive experience with my career idea.

IT WILL JUST GO IN THE TRASH CAN

The world of writing is often filled with rejection for career feminists. As a young professor in a world that constantly uses the phrase "publish or perish", I felt pressure to have publications. I would constantly send out articles to professional academic journals for publication consideration. One day as I was mailing several manuscripts, a colleague said, "Those manuscripts will just go in the trash can and no one will ever read them." That negative remark made me have doubts about my writing. I started to wonder if I was just wasting my time writing because no one would be reading my manuscripts. I am glad that I did not give up on writing because I started receiving calls from editors and had several articles published in academic journals that year. My choices on hearing the negative remark involved wanting to give up the writing of articles, or to continue seeking publications although I sometimes received rejection. It was a more positive experience to keep on writing rather than give up because of the negative remark. Career feminists face pressure and negative remarks on a daily basis that can cause discouragement in the job setting. It sometimes takes a strong will to keep the faith in what you are doing when others downplay your efforts and question your actions.

YOU'RE A FAILURE

Sometimes people let society or their families dictate whether they are going to be a success. I have met women who flunked out of high school or made bad grades. However, some women I have met have dropped out of high school, taken the GED test, and were later outstanding students in college. These women decided that despite what family and society might have told them they were determined to make something out of themselves. They did not let a low score or cutting remarks that people made stop their desire to obtain success in a career. These women became great role models to empathize with the tough situations of women in similar conditions. Their ability to change a negative situation to a positive experience is a wonderful example to other women.

NEGATIVE REMARKS THAT BACKFIRE

Sometimes career women do not realize the implications for their own careers when they are making negative remarks about another woman's career. I have seen this in young career women when they want to make a complaint about a policy or an issue. Instead of sticking to the issue or compliant they start to attack all the personality points they dislike in their female boss or female co-workers. I have even heard a young women say that she was speaking for everyone in the office. Little did she know that the only person she was speaking for was herself. All the negative remarks she made came out of her own mouth. Colleagues and bosses remember the person sending the message and the disapproving voice and mannerisms that he or she is conveying. A woman making negative remarks needs to keep them objective and to the point or issue so that they do not backfire and project her as negative and unwilling to cooperate.

USE CAUTION
WHEN SHARING PERSONAL THINGS

I think women really have to study other women to determine if they are friends or foe. The test of friendship is one that requires trust and develops over time. Sometimes women jump into sharing very important things with other women they do not really know very well. This creates problems because some women will use this personal confidential information to damage their careers. In starting a new job or career you would probably want to do a whole lot more of listening than speaking. You will discover how women in that office or organization talk about other women. You will see if they are focusing on the positive or the negative in their conversations. Chances are that if women are constantly talking about negative things in other women, they are probably saying negative things about everyone. I try to avoid negative women as much as possible. I seek friendships with women I can gain positive experiences with and women who will help me and really care about my future. Be cautious in sharing personal things until trust is developed in friendships.

REMARKS THAT ARE NOT NEGATIVE

Sometimes people just sound negative when they do not really mean to convey that impression. If the career woman is tired and depressed, she may come across cold and callous when she really does not mean to come across that way. These cold feelings may be taken the wrong way when they are not meant to be negative. Think about the time of day you are going to ask your boss for a raise or important favor at work. If you are grouchy on a Monday morning that may come across negative, even when you do not mean to sound that way. This is true if you have stayed up late at night working on a project and you have to make a group presentation the next day. If you are tired, it may have an effect on your presentation. You might respond negatively to other people's ideas or even make negative remarks because you are just worn out. To convey a more positive impression consider planning a project ahead of time to relieve stress and then get plenty of rest the night before the big presentation.

GOSSIP IN THE WORKPLACE

Gossip probably places career women into more uncomfortable situations than any other thing. Perhaps it is because gossip is in every work place around the globe. It's usually wasted words about unimportant things that end up hurting people.

Women can make great progress and accomplish twice as much if they avoid getting involved in the gossip circles of work.

CULTURAL VALUES

Differences in cultural values may have an impact on understanding the negative gossip in the workplace. When a woman takes a job in a community or a city, she may not be aware of underlying customs or traditions that have been around for a long time. For example, in some small southern communities there is a custom of spending time in circles of gossip. This is part of the culture and if the new woman employee does not participate in this gossip she may be looked upon as cold, unfriendly or even uncooperative. When going to a job interview or accepting a job transfer, it might be a good idea to examine the cultural and community values of the new location.

This happened to me as I was teaching in a small college nestled in rural Texas. The department's office space was very small and we were in close proximity of each other. The department was composed of all women with college degrees. I would sit in my tiny office writing and composing articles to submit for publication. It was often difficult to concentrate because at any given time three or four of my colleagues would be out in the front office gossiping about students and other campus personnel. I really tried to ignore it for the longest time and go ahead with my writing goals and plans for career advancement. I thought that if I was acting like a professional and doing my job, these other women would look at me as a role model. Instead of looking at me as a role model, my female colleagues saw me as cold and callous for not participating in the gossip that made up a large part of the cultural values in that small southern community.

OLD FRIENDS

It is also very difficult to break into some groups of women in organizations who have been friends for years and may even have established cliques. These women often have stayed in the same jobs for years. These "old friends" have seen young women come and go and they have established their territories. Many "old friends" in the workplace have been through emotional experiences such as family break-ups, deaths, births, and an array of events that have bonded them together emotionally. Because these friendships have taken years to build there are may be underlying issues that a new female employee would not recognize or have any idea about what is happening. It's part of the workplace that women should seek to understand and appreciate. It's important in understanding office politics and how some women can get things accomplished, while others have little success.

This is one area that I believe women and men have similar experiences. For years, people talked about the "good ole boy's network." It was obvious that deals were made over a game of golf and younger family members were offered jobs because of their parents connections with "old friends". This is not a "man thing" because women are in positions of power and they have their own "old friends." It will be interesting to see how the make-up of major corporations and organizations change as women are in these very powerful positions. A number of interesting research projects could be developed on understanding the cliques and exclusive old friends of women in power positions. There is curiosity about how women involve their "old friends" in decision making, recommendations for job advancement, committee appointments, nominations for awards, and general networking in professional settings.

COMPETITION AND GOSSIP

One possible explanation for negative gossip might be that of competition in the workplace. Since many occupations are extremely competitive, there seems to be a mentality among some women to destroy the competition through gossip. This is usually done by breaking all the rules and doing everything possible to destroy another woman's career.

The gossip may take place by starting informal rumors or tattle tailing to the boss about another colleague. Some women try to make other woman colleagues look bad so they will look better in the eyes of the boss. It is an underhanded thing to try to put down the credibility of the woman colleague. The woman spreading the gossip and lies may feel it builds her expertise and knowledge up by cutting down another woman in the organization. The gossip may be presented in a sly and suggestive way. For example, the person spreading the gossip may simply miss-communicate facts or give inadequate details about an event that occurred. This causes the person hearing the gossip to have doubts and concerns about a woman in the organization. The boss may then question the female employee about her actions.

In competitive situations for women, office gossip sometimes turns into sabotaging another woman's career. This is very distressing for me. Career feminists have worked hard to move up the career ladder. Many of them have gone to college for years, taken specialized job training, and spent hours developing successful careers. It is disheartening to think that there are women, and men, who intentionally create gossip to destroy women's careers and sabotage their job positions. This negative behavior shows the weak character of some people in our society. As a woman who has worked in professional settings, I have become aware of gossip and the women who spread it. I want to know the motive of the person who is coming to share negative gossip with me. I feel that cutting down other women to build yourself up is a negative and destructive way to get ahead.

CAREER DESTROYERS

One negative aspect of my career has been what I will term as encounters with female career destroyers. I am sure there are men who gossip, although my personal experiences have been with women. I pose the question of, "Why would someone intentionally try to destroy another woman's career?" I feel there are several reasons career destroyers do this.

First, no matter how nice you are to people, there will usually be someone in your workplace who does not care for you. Some colleagues will openly tell you they do not like you, while others are very inconspicuous and quiet about what they do not like about you. This is why career feminists must be cautious about who and what they are talking about in professional settings. Some career destroyers sit in their ivory towers and enjoy looking down and laughing at you as you struggle up the career ladder. Career destroyers sometimes act out of jealousy. The person may be jealous of you and insecure about his or her position. As a result, the career destroyer may give you an undeserved, low evaluation for job performance. Your first response will probably be that this is unfair and you will not understand the low rating.

Career feminists can try to remove themselves from a negative situation and surround themselves with more positive workers. However, this is not always possible if the career destroyer is your boss. The woman might try to work on projects more independently so that she is not in constant contact with the career destroyer. Sometimes talking with the career destroyer informally will help bring things out in the open to address the situation. If that does not work the woman may want to put her concerns in writing and suggest some ideas for a more workable solution. In most work situations, there is at least one person who really does not care for our best interests. Career feminists must confront both the positive and negative aspects of the work environment.

IS HONESTY ALWAYS THE BEST POLICY?
SOMETIMES

Growing up in a rural Oklahoma family, I was taught the simple belief that "honesty was the best policy." I have a strong human relations background that wants people to be honest with me so it would be natural that I would want to be honest with other people. However, I have learned that working with some women there is a problem with being totally open and honest. The problem is that some women take the information that you honestly share with them and use it against you in a negative way. Career women need to be aware of this as they confront daily work situations.

I want to remind you that if something works for someone else it might not work for you. This is because there are so many personality types in the working world. One female employee may make a request and it will be approved without question. Another female employee could make the same request and get non-approval. This simply implies that a boss may be inconsistent in how he or she responds to employees. Therefore, if you notice that your boss is inconsistent in the way he or she treats employees you might want to be cautious about being so open and honest with him or her. You may also want to be cautious if you think the boss might use the information against you in the future. The following is a personal example of how being honest with my female boss hurt me in the workplace:

It was one of those sticky situations that many women get into everyday. I had a two day job interview out of state and needed to ask for two days off work to go out of town. I could call in sick or just be honest with my boss. As a young professional woman I thought being honest with my boss would be the best. I told her that I really did not think I would get the job but, that I wanted to try to better my career since I was selected as a finalist for the position. I was not ready for the horrible reaction I received from this honest request. My boss told me that if I went to the interview that she would give me a bad recommendation on all future jobs. She also told me that I was not a team player anymore and that I was not being loyal to my present position by seeking outside employment. I went to the interview, but was not offered the out-of-state position. I was totally devastated by the negative reaction and how I was treated by being honest. I had put my present job in a threatening position and lost a valuable job recommendation that I thought I really needed in my early career years. I created a negative work situation for myself in my quest to be honest. I think back on those situation years later and how it may have turned out differently if I had just called in sick or rescheduled the job interview during a semester break. I survived this experience when six months later I was chosen as a finalist for another job interview. This time I did not tell anyone about the interview. I had a great interview and was offered a promotion with a ten thousand dollar raise.

In retrospect, I believe honestly is still very important to my character and my abilities. However, the degree to which I reveal my honest thoughts and feelings is somewhat dependent on the person I am sharing the information with and how they use it. If I get extremely negative feedback on ideas and remarks that I feel are truly valuable and important I will tone back the degree to which I share honest feelings and thoughts. It makes me feel more secure to know that I can share honest feelings and thoughts with people I trust and who truly care about me.

CONCLUSION

When women face negative remarks in the workplace, they have a choice with what to do with the information. They can become discouraged and give up on their career goals or they can take the negative remark and turn it into a positive experience in the following ways:

CHALLENGE-See the negative remark as a challenge to prove the person wrong and accomplish your goal. This works for me as long as the goal is realistic for me. If I have unrealistic expectations, the challenge may never be accomplished. For example, if someone says, "You will never finish the book," I can write the book and prove them wrong. On the other hand, if I tell someone I am going to write a thousand page book in thirty days, I probably would not meet the challenge because I've put an unrealistic expectation on myself. A challenge can help a woman by giving her a goal to work toward and a spark in a new direction of interest.

REDIRECTION-Take the negative remark and change your direction to a more appropriate goal or a more suitable and realistic experience. Sometimes a negative remark will cause us to rethink our situation. For instance, a woman who is told that her typing skills are slow and that her production level is low may redirect her career interest in jobs where dexterity is not a high priority. It does not mean that her typing skills are not important, rather that she needs to look at occupations where typing is not the major focus of the job. The woman redirects her career choice from the negative remark and seeks an occupation that better suits her skills and needs.

POSITIVE RESPONSE-When I work with people who are constantly giving me negative remarks, I try to get away from them, by seeking helpful, positive people in the workplace. Positive people motivate me to do my best and reach my goals. Women should not forget to use humor to see the lighter side of negative issues. A joke or some light hearted comment can downplay a negative remark and provide a more positive response. If women are feeling good about the work environment and laugh at the little things, a positive workplace will result.

CHAPTER SEVEN
THE REALIZATION OF FEMINISM

It has taken me years but I have slowly begun to understand how some women come to a realization about feminism. I have become aware of three steps of feminism realization for women. These steps were developed by observing women and watching how they came to a realization of their beliefs. This is not a time-line approach with each step happening at a certain time in life. These are not age related steps because a realization of feminism can occur at various ages throughout the life cycle. For some women, realization of feminism comes early with a strong internal message. Other women may take years to explore and discover their ideas about feminism.

The three steps of feminism realization for women are:

1. Internalization of Feminism
2. Expression of Feminism
3. Re-examination of view on Feminism

A flow chart on the following page depicts these simple steps. In this chapter I will explain these three steps and give examples of how women come to this realization of feminism.

Dr. Susan Louise Peterson's:

THREE STEPS OF
FEMINISM REALIZATION
FOR WOMEN

Internalization
of
Feminism

⇓

Expression
of
Feminism

⇓

Re-examination
of views on
Feminism

INTERNALIZATION OF FEMINISM

Women, young and old, begin to internalize images and experiences they have had with feminism throughout their lives. At family gatherings, school events, social happenings, workplace routines and a variety of other functions in our society, women are observing what people are saying to them and about them and how women act and treat each other. They are making mental inscriptions in their minds and informally noting these incidents related to feminism.

I think back to my childhood and I can remember numerous incidents where I was internalizing ideas about feminism. I was growing up in a large family that had five boys and two girls. In my early teens, I noticed disparity in the household rules and duties. The family dating rule was that the boys could go out and stay out as late as midnight, but the daughters had to be in by ten o'clock. The sisters were expected to clean the house and do the dishes after each meal while the brothers were not expected to do any house work. Even as a young teenager I began internalizing that our household system was not very fair and that there was not equality in how the sexes were treated in the family.

The issues of feminism that women internalize do not have to be real complicated. They may come from very simple everyday situations. A young professional woman running down to the dry cleaners may notice a sign on the window that shirts are laundered for ninety-nine cents. She takes a bundle of her husband's and her own shirts to get starched. The woman finds out that his shirts cost ninety-nine cents, but her shirts may cost considerably more. She internalizes that something is wrong with the way she is treated at the dry cleaners.

Another example could be the female faculty member with years of experience and honors. Surprisingly, a male faculty member fresh out of graduate school and no work experience comes to the university and his salary is equivalent or even above the female faculty member's salary. The female professor begins to internalize her observations and makes a mental note about how the institution respects her.

EXPRESSION OF FEMINISM

Once women have internalized their images and experiences of feminism, they begin to express these ideas in a variety of channels and avenues. This expression of feminism can come at a number of times and age levels throughout the life cycle. Some women may internalize a message about feminism and express it immediately, while other women may internalize a feminist issue over a long period of time before expressing it. The expression of feminism is not just expressed verbally by women. Some women write in order to put meaning into their feminist ideas. Other women may depict their feminism through art, dancing or music. The ways women express their feminism are essentially limitless.

As I mentioned earlier, I had internalized household incidents that influenced my feminist thinking by my early teens. About the age of thirteen, I began to express my feminism in our family. Needless to say, it was not taken in a positive or constructive way by my family. It all begin around the television set (something I seldom watch anymore). The television was dominated by the males in my family. On this particular night the old classic "The Sound of Music" was on for its once a year showing. As I gleefully watched Julie Andrews singing on the hillside, my brother came up abruptly and turned the television channel to his favorite show.

Immediately, my expression of feminism began to verbalize. "That is not fair," I told my mother. "The Sound of Music is on only one time of the year and the boys watch their show all the time," I said with a wish for my predicament to be resolved by my mother. My mother addressed the situation by telling me to go outside and the television remains dominated by males in that house to this very day. Luckily for me I do not live in that house any more, so my egalitarian husband

and I make our own television rules. Those small television incidents were powerful for me to express my feminism at an early age.

Expressing feminism is not always so obvious. For example, my sister Myral whom I discussed in an earlier chapter seems to have come to some realization about feminism in her late thirties. She does not use the word feminism or feminist to express or describe herself. If I asked Myral if she were a feminist she would probably say no. However, many of the things she is expressing through casual conversations and telephone discussions are the same feminist ideas I once expressed during my early twenties in college. I think Myral has internalized many feminist thoughts and ideas for years, but has just been able to express them openly in the past several years. That is why there are no age stages connected with the three steps of feminism realization. Women are internalizing and expressing their feminism at different ages and stages in the life cycle.

RE-EXAMINATION OF VIEWS ON FEMINISM

Once feminism is internalized and expressed by women, they begin to re-examine their views and ideas about feminism in relation to what they have learned about it. This is a very important part of understanding the realization of feminism because women can be introspective.

I reflect decades later on statement about women that I heard someone say years ago. I try to understand why someone would make such a prejudiced and biased statement about women. I grew up in the rural, primarily agriculture state of Oklahoma. I heard a man once say, "I do not think women should learn how to read, because they will then want a driver's license and they will run off and get a job." By re-examining my feminist views, I can see that the person who made this statement was uneducated about women and highly threatened by the idea that a woman could get a job. His focus was extremely limited to his narrow point of view about feminism. Where the statement angered me years ago, I now find that by re-examining it I can see the purpose in educating young and old people of both sexes about the realizations of feminism. In summary, if women internalized thoughts and ideas about feminism, expressed their reflections on feminism and re-examined the issues of feminism, they would gain a greater sense of realization about feminism.

CHAPTER EIGHT
SPREADING THE MESSAGE
OF FEMINISM

The message of feminism must continue to be studied in scholarly circles. With changing technology, the principles of feminism can be shared with young and old through a variety of ways. This chapter will identify ways the message of feminism can be communicated to others.

WOMEN'S STUDIES PROGRAMS

Women's studies programs and courses over the past years have been at the forefront in sharing information on feminism. Women's studies departments vary in their scope and focus as they relate back to the mission of their unique university. However, many women's studies programs have lots of common ground. Many programs study women's concerns, policy issues effecting women, historical aspects of women, women in society and the workplace, depiction of women in film, the arts and literature, and other scholarly areas related to women. Because the study of women entails many things, it is not uncommon for women's studies programs to be interdisciplinary. Faculty from several departments may work cooperatively with women's studies and develop courses specifically geared on women in a variety of fields.

The women's curriculum in many women's studies programs includes a historical look at women, an examination of changing trends for women, and predictions for women in the future combined with carefully thought out learning outcomes. The women's curriculum may specialize in certain knowledge areas that focus on a central theme unique to a university women's studies program. For example, a women's curriculum focusing on women in literature may have learning outcomes and competencies based on knowledge of selected feminist literature. Other women's studies programs that have a social focus may emphasize decision making, problem solving, strategy development, and human relations skill training in their women's studies curriculum. The women's curriculum will probably have unique features according to its specific goals and objectives. The broad features of women's studies allow more viewpoints, angles, and perspectives to be shared with others. The women's studies programs provide a positive outlook for spreading feminism.

FEMINIST RESEARCH

Feminism continues to be spread through feminist research. Feminist research is a broad term used to describe scholarly research on women and related to women's concerns. Since many women's studies programs are interdisciplinary, feminist research takes many forms and directions. Feminist researchers interested in the contemporary aspects of feminism may research present women's issues. They may also focus their research on policies and laws that are currently effecting the lives of women. Feminist researchers interested in historic research may collect information through oral history and testimonials from people on women's topics. Another feminist research method involves analyzing texts and writings on women in past documents and books. Some feminist researchers believe that by researching the past we can gain better understanding of women in the present and future times. Feminist research may entail such things as theoretical and practical questions about women, as well as research methods used to conduct and investigate in women's studies.

Some feminist researchers and women's studies philosophers explore gender expectations as part of their research. They are concerned with society's expectations about how each gender should behave and act. Gender research often begins with studies on young children as they are establishing their gender roles early in life. Women's studies professionals are often interested in studying about sexism and sex roles. They research such things as the behavior of the sexes, sex roles stereotyping, sex role development, sex role mannerisms and attitudes, and theories about sex roles. The goal of investigating sex roles is often related back to understanding the socialization of women and men. There is so much feminist research that could be done on the above topics. Just imagine the broad picture of feminist research and the numerous topics that can be explored to gain a better understanding of feminism.

The following is a brief list of topics related to feminism and women's studies that could be researched.

*dual career marriages and feminism

*women in high management positions

*the role of women in the ministry and religious organizations

*male support for feminism

*feminist attitudes of young people

*violence against women

*the role of women related to spiritual and religious writings

*development of international women's programs

*philosophical beliefs about women's studies

*ways to teach feminism to children

*administration issues in women's programs

*women's salaries and pay equity issues

*examine the core curriculum in women's studies programs

*review graduate and undergraduate programs in women's studies

*feminism and marital relationships

*the job market for women's studies graduates

*reproductive issues in feminism

*the interdisciplinary nature of women's studies programs

*college requirements in women's studies

*women's self-image

*poverty issues and feminism

*explore curriculum trends in women's studies

*identify outstanding women's programs

*analyze different types of feminism

*examine characteristics of outstanding women leaders

*explore societal attitudes about feminism

*women's influence in political positions

*feminism and the stay at home parent

*retirement concerns for women

*investigate how women are portrayed in the arts

*multicultural issues in women's studies

*philosophical definitions of feminism

*an overview of the women's movement

*pros and cons of women's liberation

*why some men speak up for feminism

*the opposition of feminism

*women and power

*the issue of pay equity and women

*an examination of feminist literature

*feminism and aggression

*feminist consciousness

*women in the political realm

*describe a feminist agenda

*national dialogues of women's issues

*a historical account of women's achievement

*special interest groups in feminism

*a look at women in the labor force

*reproductive issues for women

*waves of feminism

*friendships of women

*reforming women's policies

*women and international development

*myths about women

*changing views of feminism

*how feminism impacted society

*an examination of women's studies journals

*an overview of the women's studies discipline

*the goals of feminism

*women and voting

*organizational styles of feminism

*dividing issues of feminism

*different types of feminists

*religion and women's issues

*what is feminist therapy?

*a historical account of the women's suffrage movement

*the occupational status of women

*the biblical feminists perspective

*an explanation of the term radical feminist

*how the women's movement changed lives

*disagreements about feminism

*program development in women's studies

*attitudes of women's studies majors

*develop a historical profile of an important woman

*analyze women's behavior in novels

*write a personal account of a woman's experience

*compare and contrast the views of two women

*discuss sexism

*review a women's studies magazine or article

*profile a woman in sports

*take a critical look at women in films

*conduct an interview with a woman in a powerful position

These are just a few ideas in an endless list of feminist research topics.

COMPUTERS AND TECHNOLOGY

Feminism can now be spread rapidly through electronic technology. Computer programs and the world wide web can provide women's studies bibliographies, course outlines, book reviews, magazine articles, and lots of other information in feminist research. The area of computers and technology should be included in women's studies programs so graduates can explore new avenues of feminism and have up-to-date job market skills.

FEMINIST THERAPY

Feminist therapy involves a treatment approach that focuses on a woman's perception. It may include therapy on understanding sex role socialization, gender expectations and ideas, and the behavior of men and women. Exploring a woman's vision in feminist therapy can be a helpful remedy for improving relationships and coming to terms with a person's sex role identity.

WOMEN'S AGENDA

Feminism is also spread by women's organizations, committees, and groups that form a women's agenda which is sometimes called a feminist agenda. A women's agenda is a plan or schedule to bring greater awareness to women's issues. It may be prioritized with the most important concerns listed first. The women's agenda might include some of the following items:

-increasing women's involvement in legislative issues

-the funding of women's programs

-concerns about policies affecting women

-research activities involving women

-re-examining critical issues related to the lives of women

-pay equity issues for women in the workplace

-participating in decision making on women's issues

-involvement in groups and committees on women's policies

-identifying health care concerns for women

-input on future women's programs

Through a women's agenda, women can have input on critical issues that impact their lives. They can become change agents that speak up for the interest of women. It is believed the programs will be improved, laws will be changed, and policies will be re-examined to better women's lives.

The message of feminism is being spread and communicated in many ways. Women's studies programs have brought attention to many feminist issues. Feminist research has been and will continue to be important in exploring the past, present, and future of women. Computers and technology will continue to provide available information of feminist topics and research. Feminist therapy will play an important role in understanding women's perceptions and visions. Women's agendas will provide plans to bring greater awareness to women's issues. Even with all of these capabilities and resources there is still so many areas to explore and research on feminism. The changing nature of feminism and people's attitudes about how men and women should and do behave opens the door for continued research opportunities on feminism. It is an ongoing process to educate and enlighten society on the changing meaning of feminism.

CHAPTER NINE
CHALLENGES FOR FEMINISM

The world of feminism is constantly faced with challenges. These challenges cause feminists to address new issues affecting the lives of women and to re-evaluate continual concerns involving women. I feel challenges in the world of feminism can be positive for women. The challenges cause women to ask questions and search out new angles and trends in feminism. This inquiry opens the door for further query and research. As new curiosity arises about women, it will help to understand feminism and its changing meaning and nature. Young girls have no idea about the challenge they will face in the future. It is hard to predict new challenges as technology changes, new research is developed, and attitudes change about the sexes. There are some issues however that continue to challenge women no matter what situation plays a part in their lives. In this chapter, I will explain some of the important challenges women face in the world of feminism. These are not the only challenges that women face, but they characterize some of the major concerns. As societal views change and people's perspective about women evolve, the challenges for feminism will in time be rewritten and modified.

FAULT-FINDERS

Fault-finders are lurking around at every corner in almost every field of study. It is no different in the field of women's studies and the study of feminism. There are people out to find the faults of feminism and capitalize on any weakness or blunder the moment it occurs. These people are easy to spot because they are just waiting to antagonize anything connected to feminism and women's studies. I am not talking about constructive criticism and critical thinking about feminism that occurs often in discussions and academic circles. I am concerned with people who are not interested in learning anything new about feminism and have a very closed mind and limited focus about it.

These fault-finders often seek to catch the feminist with being inconsistent. An example of this would be a woman who demands that others call her a fir-fighter and then one day she inadvertently refers to someone as a fireman. The fault-finder is right there to inform the feminist of her inconsistent statement. His or her intention is not to do anything, but point out fault. Most women will do one of two things when they are addressed by a fault-finder. A woman can take the information and challenge the person on the spot in order to enlighten the fault-finder's point of view. She can also use the incident to become more self-informed and educated on the topic so she can respond quickly to future negative remarks from fault-finders.

Just the word feminist itself triggers negative thoughts in the fault-finder. The person may point out the faults of the feminist by name calling her as a "man-hater" or some other narrowly focused label. Many women are educated enough to quickly spot prejudice and narrow minded attitudes. They again have choices of what to do with the close-mindedness of the fault-finder. Some women would respond quickly to clarify the fault-finders position. Other women would simply ignore the person and avoid him or her if possible. Yet, some women would take the time to educate this person about feminism and its impact on our lifestyles.

Fault-finders come and go in women's lives, but the reality of the situation is that there will always be someone pointing his or her finger at feminism. Feminists must maintain their enthusiasm and positive attitude even when confronted with negative remarks from frustrated people. Feminists can address rejections and objections with a positive and upbeat attitude.

UNREALISTIC EXPECTATIONS

Many years ago, I was invited to judge the interview portion of a national beauty pageant. Let me first clarify that I am not against women competing against each other in contests for beauty, scholarship, sports, etc. Men also compete in pageants based on attractiveness and personal physique. We live in a competitive world and women compete with each other on a daily basis to get ahead in this world. What bothers me is the unrealistic expectations that society sometimes puts on young girls as they are preparing for pageants and contests.

Over anxious parents can spend thousands of dollars on self-confidence and modeling training for a young girl who does not have the physical make-up to become a top model. As a judge, I called this "over training" by the contestant's parents or coach. These parents and coaches would have the contestants so hyped up to believe they could do anything, even if it was totally an unrealistic expectation. An example of this over-training occurs often in the interview portions of pageants. Young women are often trained to believe they can be anything in the world no matter what their physical make-up might be. I am not against young women having a positive and self confident attitude when coming to an interview. I am against filling their heads with unrealistic ideas about what they can become in life.

A typical interview question asked at a state, regional or national beauty pageant might be the following: "What career do you see yourself in or basically what do you want to be when you grow up?" Before the pageant, I thought I might get responses like a doctor or a teacher. Surely, these young women would be considering typical occupations like their parents. I was totally wrong because many of these young girls had a totally distorted picture of what was ahead for them in their lives.

The answer that most of the girls gave that day was a super model. They wanted the lifestyle of the super model and they had the unrealistic expectation to believe that was in their future. Of the twenty girls I judged that day, only one realistically had the height to be a super model. I watched these five feet tall girls weighing one hundred and forty pounds talk about becoming a super model. The modeling agent seated next to me kept making comments that many of the girls would have difficulty getting beginning modeling jobs, much less a super model job.

I tried to probe deeper about this super model thing. I would mention to the pageant contestant that only a few women are selected to be super models and that if it did not work out, had they considered another occupation. I thought they might say something like, "Sure, I want to be a doctor." I was wrong again, because the girls had so much self-confidence training, they still believed that they would be a super model no matter how hard it was or what obstacles they would face. Do not get me wrong. I am a strong believer in motivation and determination. I believe many people can succeed and accomplish enormous goals by having a self-confident attitude and realistic expectations. My concern is the harm that is done by putting girls and young women in a frame of mind where they have a distorted picture of reality and unrealistic expectations of future careers. Competition for women can be healthy if there is an understanding of reality. Young girls can have fun and gain positive experiences through their friendships and competitive experiences, but they must coincide with future realistic expectations.

Society itself sometimes adds to these unrealistic expectations, especially since many young girls believe they will grow up to be thin and slender. They look at the ads in the Sunday newspaper and in hundreds of magazines that line the grocery store shelves with thin, tall women looking back at them, and yet still believe they will look this way as they grow older. I think the fashion industry partially sets this tone as they design so many clothes to fit certain types of bodies. If your body does not fit into one of these perfect sizes, you could be out of luck in finding the right outfit.

I can think of two examples where I went shopping for relatively simple clothing items. I would describe my figure as an average build. I am not skinny, but I am not obese either. I am rather somewhere in between the two sizes. The first item I went shopping for was a belt. I had not worn a belt in years, but I thought a belt would dazzle up those blue jeans that I really enjoyed wearing. A trip to the mall brought me home empty handed. To my dismay, I found that the belts hanging on the racks were meant for very tiny waists. They were not even close to fitting around my waist. I wondered if the belt manufactures believed that only small people wear belts and that women with medium or larger sizes wear only stretch or spandex type pants. I finally found two belts at a thrift store where I searched for hours. I take good care of those belts because who knows how long it will take me to find another one my size.

The second item I had trouble finding was an interview outfit that I needed shortly after college graduation. I thought it would be no problem since I knew my size. However, I had forgotten those extra pounds that I had gained during my final years of college. The jacket size was a perfect size twelve, but for the skirt I needed a size fourteen. I started to get a skirt from another hanger, when the sales consultant informed that I could not mix up the sizes on the outfits. If I did not fit into the perfect size twelve jacket and skirt, I was out of luck in getting an outfit. I could always buy a larger size if I was willing to pay someone to make alterations and help me fit the outfit. It still bothers me that clothing manufacturers have had the unrealistic expectations that women fit into perfect sizes and that their bodies are accurately proportioned to those sizes. I have to give some credit to a few clothing manufacturers who are specializing in clothes for larger women. My major complaint is the stores specializing in larger women's clothing are extremely overpriced and for women struggling to work up the career ladder, they often have difficulty paying these prices.

Our society in America has make some major strides dealing with a few of these unrealistic expectations. There are finally magazines that deal with issues that effect big and large women. These women can relate and share stories with each others about their concerns and successes. There are even beauty pageants for large and plus-size women. No one would have ever thought there would be a pageant for larger women twenty years ago. Society changes as women inform others of their successes and make efforts to set realistic expectations for our world.

I have also noticed that society seems to judge average looking women stricter than average looking men. One of my first jobs out of college was as a production assistant for television station. There was a female reporter at the station. She was a very intelligent and average looking woman. The news station received several phone calls commenting that the female reporter was ugly and had a "pig face" even though her reporting was excellent. I noticed that the male reporters who were overweight and balding did not receive those types of calls. It seemed more acceptable for the male reporters to look average than the female reporters.

Society also seems to judge fashion and appearance more harshly for women celebrities than men celebrities. A radio station in a metropolitan area wanted the listeners to call in and comment on the country music awards show that had aired on television the previous night. Probably about 95% of the calls criticized one female singer. They make negative comments about her hair, her make-up, and her clothes. I was rather surprised that no one commented about the appearance of the male county singers. I am sure there were a few men who probably did not dress their best or appear in top form. The calls centered around women and what people thought their appearance should be and the calls were very detailed about ways women could improve in their appearance. It is to be hoped that feminism will help educate people not to judge a person's character solely on how a person looks or on their physical appearance.

STEREOTYPIC BEHAVIOR

I honestly wish I could say that people's bias and stereotypes about women did not exist, but unfortunately they still exist in today's society. I feel that many people in our society are more aware of the wonderful accomplishments that women have made and have become more accepting of women in professional positions. There are always a few people whose stereotypic behaviors that make it difficult and put stumbling blocks in the way of women. This is a challenge that women have to face in day to day occupations.

I think a good example of this is seen in women who are going into the ministry. More women are attending seminaries and training to serve the world as pastor and minister of churches. Many of these women find acceptance of their beliefs and ideas while they are students at seminary, but after they enter the ministry field they see a different picture.

Young, female ministers often start out in lower paying jobs at small, rural churches as they gain experience. The problem is often members of these churches are older and are not use to having a woman serve as a minister or leader. At times there is criticism of the woman as minister based on stereotypic attitudes about women's roles. A biased person starts finding faults in the women minister and her ideas because he or she is unwilling to accept something that is non-conventional or a new idea to a community. It is still a challenge for feminism to re-educate people of women's new directions and influences on programs that enhance a greater understanding in society. The challenge of stereotypic behavior is one that women have faced in the past and will continue to face in the future.

There are also stereotypes that people have about how a feminist should act or look. Some people think a feminist has very short hair, wears no make-up, and wears army boots. There is sometimes the assumption that feminists hate men. The problem with these stereotypes is that it lumps all women with feminist beliefs into one small category. Women with diverse experiences, home environments, education and specialized training do not feel the same about all the elements of feminism. People who have a distorted image of how a feminist should act or look often confront feminists with harsh and unfair accusations. Feminists must constantly combat these false images from people with bias and negative stereotypes about women. The positive lifestyle of many feminists is a productive and important example to society.

SENSITIVITY ISSUES

A challenge that women have in understanding their feminism is dealing with sensitivity issues. This has really changed for me over the years as I have grown older. As a young single college student, I somehow had the view that being a feminist meant being strong, extremely independent, being cold hearted, and not being too emotionally attached to anything. Fifteen years later, I found out that I could be strong and independent, but I could also be warm hearted and emotionally attached to people and things. I could have feminist beliefs and still was happy, sensitive and have loving relationships with people.

I remember a young woman I met in graduate school in Oklahoma. I noticed Mary was very strong in her feminist beliefs from the classes we took together. I ran into her about eight years later as we were taking an aging seminar in Texas. I was married for eight years and in a very strong and happy relationship with my husband. I have never forgotten her words that I was looking "through rose-colored glasses" and that I had an unrealistic view of marriage to think I was going to be happy with a man. Mary was a perfect example of a young woman who thought she was immune from having a sensitive side. She felt her strength in feminism came from being tough and opposing the views of men.

Woman cannot forget that the strength of feminism comes from being understanding of people and issues that impact women's lives. As women are emphatic, they comprehend and interpret the meaning of feminism and how it relates to others in our society. The power and strength of women with feminist beliefs comes from an intensity to understand the character of people and sensitivity issues.

SELF-CONFIDENCE

A challenge for women discussing feminism is dealing with self-confidence issues. Sure it is easy to discuss feminist issues around people that agree with us or share a common goal about women with you. However, it becomes a bit more challenging to discuss feminism issues with people who totally disagree with you. As a result, some women become self-conscious about sharing information with a difficult person who lacks understanding and is uneducated about feminism. Some women chose not to engage in these battles and debates because they do not want to make mistakes and look bad in front of others. Self-confidence is important for women so that they can stand proudly to discuss the meaning and issues of feminism with others. Talking about feminism in a relaxed and comfortable way exalts a woman's self-confidence. It takes time to develop this self-confidence because women are in different stages of internalizing, expressing and re-examining their feminist beliefs.

THE CHALLENGE OF COMPETITION WITH MEN

A newspaper reporter once asked me for an opinion column in a local newspaper. He wanted to know how I felt about men and women competing against each other in basic training. I really did not have a problem with that question because I had been competing with men since I was a child. I wrote my first speech at nine years old to compete in the county 4-H contest and yes I competed against boys and girls. I showed pigs in the county fair and competed against (you guessed it) boys and girls.

I was one of the first girls in my high school to enroll in an agriculture course and join FFA (Future Farmers of America). I was the only girl in the class, but I had no problem taking welding and learning the origin of cattle, just like the boys. At the end of my freshman year, I was awarded the Star Greenhand Award for the outstanding freshman student. I not only competed with boys, but I excelled when put in competitive situations with them.

So how did I answer the reporter's question about men and women competing against each other in the military? I simply told him that men and women compete against each other in college courses and many aspects of life. After graduating, women and men apply for jobs and compete for job openings. Women spend much of their lives in competitive settings with men and therefore it is not something to be feared, but rather a challenge. The competition that men and women are placed in can turn into challenges that increase the understanding of human dignity and human weaknesses that are present for both males and females. This healthy competition can help both men and women understand their needs and abilities.

RECOGNIZING A WOMAN'S IDENTITY

It is amazing that our society still has some very old fashioned ideas about recognizing a woman's identity. My husband and I were both teachers in the same school district. We both received health benefits, but they were listed on the insurance card under my husband's social security number. I kept having trouble getting a prescription at the pharmacy with my insurance. Finally, the pharmacy technician said that the card kept coming up with an invalid birth date. The prescription would only be processed using my husband's birth date. You would think in a professional dual career society that women and men would have their own insurance identification numbers.

ONGOING CHALLENGES OF FEMINISM

The meaning of feminism changes as society develops new ideas and views and it processes information about what is acceptable or unacceptable for women. In addressing the challenges of feminism, there will always be fault-finders who see a flaw in the philosophy, and that will keep us on our toes to stay up with the pressing questions that feminists must address. Unrealistic expectations for women will be addressed as women set realistic expectations in daily life. Stereotypic behavior, sensitively issues, self-confidence practices, and competition in real life settings will continue to challenge women as they focus in on the meaning of the ever changing world of feminism. Best wishes in your search for a better understanding to feminism and all that it offers to the world.

BIBLIOGRAPHY

I have listed a few of the many books available on feminism and women's studies. These are suggested readings to explore the meaning of feminism and women's issues.

McKenna, Elizabeth Perle. *When Work Doesn't Work Anymore: Women, Work, and Identity*. New York, NY: Delacorte Press, 1997

Newman, Leslea. *Somebody to Love*. Chicago, IL: Third Side Press, 1991.

Peters, Joan K. *When Mothers Work: Loving Our Children Without Sacrificing Our Selves*. Reading, Mass: Addison-Wesley, 1997

Rose, Nancy E. *Workfare or Fair Work: Women, Welfare and Government Work Programs*. New Brunswick, NJ: Rutgers University Press, 1995.

Stanley, Autumn. *Mothers and Daughters of Invention*. Blue Ridge Summit, PA: Scarecrow Press, 1993

Thomas, Gillian. *A Position to Command Respect: Women and the Eleventh Britannica*. Blue Ridge Summit, PA: Scarecrow Press, 1993.

VanArsdall, Nancy. *Coming Full Circle*. Chicago, IL: Third Side Press, 1996.

Wyman, Andrea. *Rural Women Teachers in the United States*. Blue Ridge Summit, PA: Scarecrow Press, 1996.

SUBJECT INDEX

ABOUT THE AUTHOR

Susan Louise Peterson has written numerous articles on the topic of women and higher education. She wrote this book out of her desire to explore the meaning of feminism. Susan has a broad educational back ground and describes herself as an educator, a sociologist and a writer. She lives in Las Vegas, Nevada with her dual career husband, Alan.